John Macleod

Elijah

Or, the spiritual vision

John Macleod

Elijah
Or, the spiritual vision

ISBN/EAN: 9783337424473

Printed in Europe, USA, Canada, Australia, Japan

Cover: Foto ©Lupo / pixelio.de

More available books at **www.hansebooks.com**

OR,

THE SPIRITUAL VISION.

BY

JOHN MACLEOD,

OF CULKEIN.

[FOR PRIVATE CIRCULATION.]

1882.

[ENTERED AT STATIONERS' HALL.]

TO THE RIGHT HONOURABLE
WILLIAM EWART GLADSTONE,
Prime Minister of England.

Had I the wit to praise
Thy worth in measured lays,
As Thou hast merit and true manliness,
Then might I wake a song
Whose echoes would prolong
The memory of England's mightiness,
All mirrored in a single Type,—
In Thee, O Patriot Sire! in Grace and Wisdom ripe!

Thine are the Royalty
And peerless Sovereignty
Of men who rule by higher right than Kings!
Whose words from early youth
Are as the seals of Truth,—
Whose Empire over Man and Nature springs
From Virtues native to the mind,—
Celestial dowries free, eternal, unconfined!

Like him of whom I sing,
Fearless of priest or king,
As loyal to the Truth that makes us free;
Thy words like levin fire
Have struck false creeds in ire,
And scattered all the clouds of sophistry
Which hung around the awful Shrine
Of the most ancient Laws of Majesty Divine!

And therefore do I pray
On each returning day,
That Thou mayest long enjoy that fruit of Age,—
Love, Honour, and Renown,
The brightest earthly Crown
Bequeathed to man in rightful heritage;
And that the sunset of thy days
May still compel the World's admiring gaze!

March, 1882.   JOHN MACLEOD.

PREFACE.

The struggle between Good and Evil, between Light and Darkness, is perhaps the oldest IDEA of Dramatic Action, and yet it is one that is always new to every man " as he cometh into the world."

This moral conflict is indeed the grand mystery of life; and as every thinking individual must unseal the mystery in some shape or another for himself, it is clear that no subject can have such absorbing interest for the majority of mankind as that which concerns the trials and perplexities, the defeats and failures of human life.

A man's master passion will certainly reveal itself in his life. The Vision of the Soul, whatever it may be, can only arise from the affections; for the heart can only *see* what it *loves*.

In the following Drama I have endeavoured to unfold this leading IDEA, and to represent it under various aspects.

AHAB, and JEZEBEL also, had to pass through the " horror of great darkness " as well as ELIJAH; but the master-passion and the vision of the Prophet were very different from those of the King.

ELIJAH suffered as a witness to truth in a world of falsehood. He " grieved for griefs which were not his own," and bore the burden of the sins of Israel. This was the crown of thorns he had to wear in common with the most royal spirits of the human race; but his master-passion sustained him, and gained for him the victory. His intense sympathy for mankind, and his all-absorbing love to God, satisfied the longings of his heart, glorified his life, and made him feel the nobleness and immortality of *being*.

The master-passion of AHAB, on the other hand, was mere worldly ambition without regard to the sufferings of humanity. The possession of the starry universe could not satisfy the cravings of such an empty soul. Hence the misery of his self-consciousness, and the impossibility of loving, or of delighting, in anything good and noble outside himself. Freedom from the curse of Self was therefore impossible to him, for "as a man thinketh in his heart, so is he."

JEZEBEL, again, may be regarded as a type of those who seek happiness in what are called the "pleasures" of this world. The emotions she craved for, and cultivated, were such as spring from the enjoyment of the lower passions; and these, fed by the gross ritual of her religion, took fire in the region of her imagination, making it a very pandemonium. She, indeed, made evil her good, by making it "religious" and "divine." The same has been done in Europe since the time of JEZEBEL. The danger of every religion lies in the effeminate ease with which the most *human* emotions, not to use a stronger expression, are converted into what its votaries are pleased to call "divine love."

Now, as all dramatic actions appeal to our common humanity, so the conflict of life, with all its sorrows and tragic narratives, makes us *one* in sympathy as well as *one* in Song. Whatever our sorrows, sufferings, defeats or failures may be, other men have experienced the same before us. This consideration makes the trials of life more tolerable:

"For whensoe'er a man observes his fellow
Bear wrongs more grievous than himself has known,
More easily he bears his own misfortune."

DRAMATIS PERSONÆ.

AHAB,—King of Israel.

JEZEBEL,—His Queen.

ELIJAH,—The Prophet.

AZRIEL,—The Spirit of Light.

TYPHON,—The Spirit of Darkness.

ELDERS,—Chorus.

PRIESTS OF BAAL,—Chorus.

PRIESTS & VESTALS OF ASHTORETH,—Chorus.

TAMAL
SINADAB } Priests of Ashtoreth.
ISHTOL

ANGELS,—Chorus.

Elijah;

or,

The Spiritual Vision.

ACT I.—ELIJAH AT CHERITH.

SCENE I.

A Hall in the Palace of JEZREEL. *Time—Evening.*

Enter AHAB.

AHAB. Where in the register of human life
　　　Have youth and hope fulfilled their promises?
　　　The noblest actions we have purposed rearing
　　　In the first glow of manhood's golden prime,
　　　Are checked by intervention of the Gods,
　　　Or moulded to the ends they have decreed.
　　　The fairest flowers of fancy's early bloom
　　　Are those that wither soonest in our sight;
　　　And that which seems at first a Paradise,
　　　Is found to be a barren, dreary waste!
　　　A King, and yet not happy! Wherefore not?
　　　Because this life is but an idle dream,
　　　A vanity!—the wisest so regarded it—
　　　An empty bubble, bursting as it forms,

Blown from the confines of mysterious void,
To mock us, and to leave us still perplexed!
What evil have I done that I should be
The scapegoat and the victim of the gods?
I once believed there was a Power above
Which fortified the righteous in their strife
Against the vulgar vices of the world;
But sage experience in the ways of man
Has taught me this, that destiny depends
On more than Moses wrote or David sang.
If I had counsel at my own begetting,
I should be now the greatest saint on earth;
Then why has He, who claims all power, not made
Me so? O God! why hast Thou made me thus?
Art Thou mine enemy, or am I Thine?
Vile dust am I, and thus by Thee compounded!
Then take it to Thyself, and new-create
A nobler handiwork than Ahab is!
The final cry of all heroic men
Is but an echo of the royal groan—
"My God! my God! why hast Thou forsaken me!"

(Hears Music at a distance.)

These tones were wont to elevate my soul,
And bring me back the visions of my youth;
But now they sound as harsh as the last trump!

(Enter Jezebel.)

There is no power in sweet sounds to waken
The transports of this heart to noble ends.

Jez. Great King! this heavy mood does not accord
With our high festival of wit and song.
The wine which cheers the hearts of god and man
Now speaks divinely on the lips of those
Whose sacred office is to banish care!
And yet a cloud hangs o'er thy royal brow
Whereon the glory of the godlike son
Of Ashtoreth, was wont to play!

Ahab.   Sweet Queen!
If all were bright as thou, and true as bright,

        This world would be a paradise of joy—
        Another Eden of celestial bliss!

JEZ. Thine is the melancholy cast of mind
        Deep wrought in high aspirings after power.

AHAB. Dear Jezebel, I know not how it is,
        But in the rearward of our merry feasts
        I feel a darkening terror pressing on
        Foreboding ruin even to our throne!
        Whence doth this shadow fall I know not; yet
        It is more real to my state of mind
        Than armèd hosts confronting me in fight.

JEZ. Our kingdom is secure;—the Syrian hosts
        Can ne'er confront our arms, so strong allied
        With Judah, Tyre and Zidon!

AHAB.   Syrian hosts!
        I fear not them with all their pointed steel;
        When warlike chariots mow harvests of death
        On bloody fields of desolating War,
        And battering swords on sounding helms respond,
        Then princely Ahab's in his element!
        Ha, Jezebel! 'tis not the fear of *Man*
        That shakes my spirit thus. Ah, no! sometimes
        The sudden images of vanished things,
        Sometimes the innate sense of coming ill,
        Flash o'er the haunted heart and bid it pause!

JEZ. That Gileadite,—that water-lapping dog,*
        Has barked his curse, and Ahab's brow is dark.
        Fie, fie, my lord! it never shall be said
        That Ahab trembles when a Tishbite howls!
        Let him consort with beasts in mountain caves,
        And rant his blasphemy on desert winds!

AHAB. And yet his curse has fallen on our land—
        There is no rain! This Gileadite may be
        A prophet of the murmurs of my heart!

JEZ. Your mind is over-sensitive, my lord.
        The blasphemy of rude and vulgar men,

---

* JUDGES, VII., 5.

            To whom the Beauty in religious Art
            Is but a sealèd chapter in the Book of Life,
            Should merit scorn, not grave and sober thought!
            A prophet—he! of what? The golden calf—
            The borrowed idol of Egyptian gold,
            The Apis of the brute sense worshippers
            Of Nile! Blind prophets are they all, and false—
            Who feed on dreams and hunger when they wake,
            Who talk of Paradise, and live in caves,
            Of angels also, and consort with beasts!

AHAB.   They think life more real when it runs
        In currents counter to the common faith.

JEZ.   Life is an art which pleases best when best
        It feigns the truth; and he alone can please
        The common herd of men whose life is set
        Fair but illusively before their eyes;
        For nothing charms the soul of man so much
        As that which seems to be reality,
        And is not so.

AHAB.   Fair Jezebel, my soul's delight!
        Thy graces charm the dusky brow of night!

JEZ.   But by the light of God, Elijah dies.
        Or to amuse our friends with better sport,
        I will deprive him of his evil sight;
        And like another Samson, shorn of strength,
        He shall be made the helpless butt of scorn,—
        Divining oracles as we may list!

AHAB.   Thou hast the genius to rebuke the proud,
        Or gild with roseate hues dark sorrow's cloud!
        Then let the damsels with their timbrels play,
        And banish care from Pleasure's flowery way!
        Let Beauty wait on Pleasure, Wine on Mirth;
        Except for lovers' rapture, what were earth!

                (Embracing the QUEEN.*)*

JEZ.   Aye, what indeed, but to be thus!
        Then follow me, my lord;

This night is sacred to our Heavenly Queen,*
Whose festival is now begun.

[*Music at a distance.   Exeunt* KING *and* QUEEN.

SCENE II.—AHAB'S FESTIVE HALL.

Enter PRIESTS OF ASTARTE *and* VIRGINS, *singing in Chorus.*

CHORUS.†

Of all my ways
  Be thy sweet grace the goal;
Of all my days
  Thine, Lady,‖ the control!
I fain would raise
Life, prayer and praise
  To Thee,—Oh, cleanse my soul!
Great faith is mine
  In Thee, Lady, in Thee;
For love benign
  Still fills these eyes for me;
While thus they shine
I'll ne'er repine,
  Whate'er my woes may be.
  Star of the sea,
Fountain and spring of light,
  That set'st us free
From all the fears of night;
  In misery
  I call on Thee,
Look down from Heaven's height!

Enter KING *and* QUEEN, *and take their seats in state.*

---

* Astarte.
† This chorus is taken *verbatim* from the Spanish.
‖ Astarte, Queen of Heaven.

Strophe.

High on his mighty throne,
In majesty alone,
Our sovereign lord the king
Shall hear the virgins sing
A song of praise,
In measured lays,
   To Baal, God of light!
And to the Heavenly Queen,
Who is, and aye hath been
   The life of all the earth, and Love's delight!
Nor less to thee, dear god of truth,
   Bright-eyed Adonis, shall the hymn ascend
   From virgin lips, and blend
Immortal beauty with thy never fading youth!

Antistrophe.

Sweep the harp and swell the chorus,—
Youth and beauty will adore us
   At the altar of our love.
Wine and garlands we will bring Her,
Our enraptured souls will sing Her
   Psalms of praise throughout the grove!
Hence, away with sullen sorrow,
   Drown it in a cup of wine;
Gods provide for cares to-morrow,
   Let this golden hour be mine!
Sweet the groves of sacred myrtle
   In the hour of eventide,
When the gentle wooing turtle
   Sings, "My love, with me abide!"

NOTE.—The worship of Astarte was at one time so licentious that its "ritual" could not be described by a modern writer without offence. Indeed, all religions which inculcate the worship or adoration of goddesses or queens of heaven have a powerful tendency to enervate the character, and to corrupt the moral and spiritual life of man or woman at its fountain head. I believe that *Mariolatry*, in the dark and middle ages, was very much the same as the worship of Astarte, in Phœnicia, and of Venus in ancient Rome; but this is a subject rather too delicate to be roughly handled. It is enough to say that as the fairest things are the most loathsome in decay, so religion, when it degenerates into sexual emotions, is the most pernicious growth of the human mind.

Sweeter still a maiden's blushes
   Than the scenes of earth and sky,
When the fire of passion rushes
   Through the heart and lights the eye!
He, the ills of life despising,
   Shall be deemed the brave and free,
Who enjoys to rapture rising
   Love's delight and ecstasy!
Every love-throb has its pleasure,
   Every virgin has her charm,—
Nature bubbles up her treasure
   From her bosom bright and warm.
Hence, away with care and sorrow,
   Drown them in a cup of wine;
Gods provide for us to-morrow,
   Let this present hour be mine!

AHAB. Mark how, when music swells in airy waves
Of harmony, the heart as lightly sits
Upon the viewless pinions of these sounds
As if it were a spirit, body free.

JEZ. Such heart-inspiring strains
Might re-awake the dead,
Or animate the hills
With all their purling brooks
With felt intelligence
To lisp the name of Love!
Yet these ethereal tones
Move not the soul of Jezebel
To greater ecstasy
Than Ahab's voice so tuned as it is now!

AHAB. Most gentle queen,
Outrivalling the shy gazelle
In grace of form
And love-compelling eye!
Thou hast thyself a tongue
Whose cunning melody,
And magic spell of song,
Might hold in ravishment
The ears of savage things.

CHORUS.   The virgin queen
                 Serenly smiling,
              In silver sheen,
                 Love's hour beguiling,
              Invites each maid
                 And gallant boy
              Who ever prayed
                 For lover's joy,
              To feed the flame,
                 Bright burning ever,
              On altar's raised
                 In great Astarte's name
              Whose fame
                 Endures for ever!
              She is the fairest fair,
                 The goddess of all love!
              Who sheds her lustre rare
                 On all who faithful prove.
              She fructifies the earth
                 With gracious dews distilling;
              And smiles on every birth
                 Of tender passion thrilling.
              She spins the thread of life,
                 From age to age enduring;
              Composing all the strife
                 In bonds of love alluring!
              Oh, praise our Virgin Queen,
                 Ye vestals of Jezreel,
              As in her light serene
                 Her voiceless spells ye feel!

AHAB.   Kind friends of Zidon, hear;
        The Queen returns you thanks, and drinks you health.

JEZ.   My faithful Counsellors, and men of God,
        I pledge you in this sacred cup of love;
        Then swear by me, who am your gracious queen,
        That vengeance, dear to the immortal gods,
        Shall swiftly overtake our enemy,
        Elijah—prophet of the golden calf!

Priests.   We swear by thee, and by the gods above!
          O Baal, hear!
Jez.   Enough; his doom is sealed!
          Now let the virgins and the priests attend
          The altars of Astarte in the grove,
          That so she may relent, and visit us
          With fructifying showers and heavenly dews,
          As late she did in Zidon, graciously
          In answer to our Father's* intercession.
          [*Exeunt* King *and* Queen; Priests *and* Maidens
          following.
Priests. Wilt thou go to the woodland with me,
          Dear maid, while the roses are blowing;
          Fair visions of love for to see,
          In ethereal fires bright glowing?
Virgins. I will go to the woodland with thee,
          To the grove where the altar is burning;
          Bright visions of love for to see,
          In the flame of Astarte, earth spurning!

SCENE III.

A Grove with an Altar burning in the midst. Priests *and* Damsels *singing and playing as they dance round the Altar.*

Virgins. The flame leaps high,
            It seeks the sky,
              Astarte's ancient dwelling;
            And every beat
            Of light and heat
              Inspires the heart love-welling!
Priests. Then round we go,
            Warm in the glow
              Of vestal flame ascending;
          * Ethbaal, King and high priest of Zidon.

     Our pulses beat
     With sacred heat
      As soul with soul is blending!

VIRGINS. Oh, goddess fair,
     Now hear our prayer,
      Send down reviving showers!
     Then shall we praise
     Thy grace always,
      Within these sacred bowers!

PRIESTS. Lo, her orb bright over Carmel
      Throbs with living ecstasy,—
     Earnest of her loving presence
      In the rites we sanctify!

CHORUS. Hark, I hear her voice resounding
      Through the azure vault of night;
     And I see her harp suspended
      With its glancing chords of light!
     Queen eternal, be thou gracious,
      Hear and answer us in peace;
     In thy loving act of mercy
      Bid the curse of famine cease!

ORACULAR RESPONSE.

The virgin goddess hears
 Your cries approving,—
Your sighs and vows and tears,
 Her heart deep moving;
And in the sacred form
 Of holy passion,
Accepts what you transform
From guilty fashion
To acts of love divine,
Self-sacrifice, surrender—
Great Nature's Law!
Without the flaw
 Of prurient depravity;
Although some men
Of curious ken
  Distinguish Love and Charity!

Is not this teeming world
   Of Earth and Air and Ocean
A witness to Astarte's reign
   In every pulse of feeling and emotion?
Her banner is unfurled
O'er the wide empire of the mighty Main,
Whose bosom swells with rapture as she looks
Down from her throne upon its placid face,
Love-conscious of the parent of its myriad brood
The goddess hears your song;
For she is Queen of harmony,
And ever weaving living forms
Of beauty, out of sight and sound
That can delight the heart of man;
And in the ravishment of her employ
See how her tears like Orient pearls
Bespangle every blade and make it smile.
Rejoice, O Virgins, in your heavenly Queen,
Who turns the barren into fruitful soil—
Creating, energising, vivifying,—
While rapt in the delight of life-begetting
All living creatures sing around her throne!

   [*Exeunt* PRIESTS, &c., *and disappear in the recesses of the Grove.*

SCENE IV.

ELIJAH *is discovered at the mouth of a Cave near the Brook Cherith. Time—Early Dawn.*

ELIJAH (*addressing the Morning Star*).
   Bright eye of Dawn, clear-purged in heaven's light!
   Thou flaming Herald of the greater Majesty,
   All hail! To thee Elijah shall look up,
   And from thy ministrations learn
   To scatter far beyond his mortal sphere

A light of a diviner radiancy,
Which eyes yet uncreated shall behold,
And bless Jehovah, Fountain Spring of Light!
O Light and Strength of Israel!
Thou Living Source of my immortal hopes,
To Thee I bend my will, and consecrate
My life. Disperse the clouds that overhang
My inward vision, and obscure my path;
So may I stumble not or fall away,
But gaze undazzled on Thy Holiness,
Till my too restless spirit, passion-purged,
Shall shine before Thee as this star of heaven.
Then might I rest in this vast solitude,
In calm communion with the soul of things,
And reck not when my spirit took its flight
Unto the bosom of the Infinite.
Alas, for me there is nor peace nor rest;
The burden of my mission, feebly borne,
Now crushes out my love and now my faith,
Until my being suffers an eclipse!
Oh, fearful contemplation, thus to live
In loneliness, and isolation pent,
When in the visitation of Thy Spirit
A mighty impulse stirs my sinking heart
To swelling purposes of WOULD and COULD;
Anon to sink in noisy hollowness,
Exhausted—baffled by the barrier
Of a whole people armed against Thy Truth!
But still Elijah shall look up to Thee,
Who mak'st the sun to shine on all alike!
O teach me then to love what Thou hast loved,
That I may have possession in Thy life,
And minister to those who sit in darkness!
Alas, what light or love do I possess?
What gentle virtue rules my heated soul?
Instead of these I nurse a wasting sorrow—
A raging fire that blasts but leadeth not!
The land is cursed; and now returns the curse
Upon myself, and those who trusts in Thee!
The poor and innocent endure it all,

While Ahab still exults in revelry!
The birds of heaven now avoid my sight,
And Cherith mocks my thirst with burning stones!

(TYPHON, *an evil spirit, suddenly appears before* ELIJAH.)

TYPHON. All hail, Elijah! Censor of mankind!

ELIJAH. And of myself! but yet I know not thee!

TYPHON. I am the Genius of yonder star,
Whose influence thou hast invoked!

ELIJAH. I know no Genius but *His* who made the star!

TYPHON. Thou knowest not my name; but sympathy,
And kindred high pursuits discover friends,
Who might erewhile be strangers to each other.

ELIJAH. Art thou a servant of the living God?
A Prince thou must be——

TYPHON. Yea, a Prince I am,
And older in His service than thou art!
This earth He made for me, to be my stage
Of high and mighty actions, man-confounding;
And in the varied acts of my employ
I've conquered Faith, and hardened royal hearts
That they might blindly follow their intent
Against the clearest light of God himself—
To perish in confusion of their crimes!
Nay, more: full oft I've been, as thou may'st know,
A lying spirit in prophetic mouths,
To flatter vanity, perplex the wise,
And make the purpose of Jehovah prosper!

ELIJAH. A lying sprite! Thou thing of evil, hence!

TYPHON. Ha, ha! Thou art but young in our intrigues,
And knowest not the secret of His government!
I stand before His Throne!——

ELIJAH. Away, foul fiend!
Avaunt, thou false accuser of the Just!

TYPHON. Not so! In me behold His minister,
Who executes His lofty purposes,—
As thou dost now! Hast thou forgot the flood,

    The fiery hail of Sodom, and the plagues
    That swept the Throne of Egypt into Hell?
    In all the Councils of His inner Court
    I am the chief adviser!—witness Job!

ELIJAH.   What, baffled fiend!
    Hast thou not yet been taught the bitter truth
    That thou canst naught destroy of earthly things
    Save thine own work? Away to Jezebel,
    And her Zidonian priests; that rebel brood
    Will lend a willing ear to blasphemy!
    Think not, vain tempter, I am ignorant
    Of sin!——

TYPHON.   Of sin! Ah, no, my friend!
    Behold this desolation thou hast made —
    And by the power I lent thee for the time—
    That neither rain, nor tender dew shall wait
    Upon the labours of the husbandman;
    Or quench the thirst of dying man or beast,
    Till I shall set the wheels of Nature free,
    Now bound in curses dark!—my curse, not thine;
    For I am prince of all the elements,
    And of the hidden springs of mortal life!

   (He offers ELIJAH *a cup of sparkling clear water.)*

    But take this cup; it will assuage thy thirst,
    Abate thy fever, and restore thy strength!

ELIJAH. To die were nothing; but to live by thee
    Were death indeed! Poor shallow fool! and lost!

TYPHON. And what art thou? An outcast in this wild—
    Despised of man, forsaken by thy God,
    Alone, unfriended, persecuted, lost!
    And yet thou would'st be great—King, priest, and
     all!
    Why waste thy life in making caves resound
    With high discourse on those ETERNITIES?
    That kindling eye of thine is fit to rule,
    If thou would'st take this world for what it is,—

A den of thieves—a nursery of lust!
But such as thou would'st make it—all Elijahs!
Ha, ha! A barren wilderness—a theatre
Of stormy rants against your fiend the Devil!
Say, who would care to witness such a scene,
Save the proud spirit of your common hate—
The great Archangel who has long defied
The everlasting thunder of his wrath,
In whom Elijah vainly puts his trust!
Thou hast the will but not the power to crush—
Whilst I have both! Then follow me, and I
Will set thee on a throne of royalty
Victorious! Command the fire to fall,
And quick as thought JEZREEL shall lie a heap
Of blackened ashes and sulphureous ruins,
As Sodom and Gomorrah did of old!

ELIJAH. It were a victory too dearly bought
That would deprive me of all good! False fiend,
Fair promises of freedom didst thou give
To guileless and unfallen Innocence!
To me thy counsel, dark as is the scowl
Upon thy thunder-blasted brow,
Is hateful as the source from which it springs.
Great power thou hast, ever devoid of good;
Great knowledge also, but of evil chief:
Thy crown is forged in Hell, and darkness shoots
From every ray of its circumference!

TYPHON. Yet am I free! My power is not subjected—
For who can dare dispute my sovereignty?
Behold yon airy region without bound
Bespangled with innumerable stars—
Peopled with worlds, each brighter than this earth—
These are the fields of my victorious acts;
Yet though those suns were quenched, and all the orbs
Were blasted out of space, I could create
A universe for God more fair than this—
With less of sin! Wouldst thou not rather, then,
Pay homage to a prince whose sovereignty
Is undisputed over all thou seest,

     Than thus to be immured in caverned rocks,
     Or wander beggarly from door to door,
     Loud railing, like an ass, against the times?

ELIJAH. I envy not thy freedom, nor thy crown,
     Both cursed alike! For in that free self-will,
     That baneful lure of all unfaithful spirits,
     There lies the deepest, lowest servitude,—
     A servitude more hopeless far
     Than that of bonds, chains and imprisonment.
     Thou hast no choice but in variety
     Of evil deeds; thy freedom holds thee thralled,
     In one eternal circle void of light,
     Where envy, hate and scorn, like scorpion whips,
     Lash thee, unto thyself a slave! Avaunt!
     Or with the fire thou challengest me to wield,
     I'll hurl thee blackened to the pit of Hell!

TYPHON. Ha! We shall see who can the thunder wield,
     And shake the mountain with its clamorous tongue.
     Farewell! At Horeb* we will meet again.

    [TYPHON *disappears in a lurid flame, whence a chorus
     of evil spirits is heard.*

1st SPIRIT. Prince of the world, all hail!
     Let not the light prevail,
    But with thy shadow cover up the day!

2nd SPIRIT. Outstretch thy mighty wing,
     And blast each living thing,
    That rills may cease to flow and springs to play!

3rd SPIRIT. Let Cherith cease to lave his bed,
    And ravens croak their curses on Elijah's head!

ALL.   On the viewless air careering,
     Haste we to the halls of mirth,
    Where the sons of pleasure rearing
     Altars to the Joy† of Earth,
    Quaff the wine cup to Adonis,
    To the hero who alone is

 ' At Horeb: that is the Mount of God. This will be the greatest of all temptations.
    † *Astarte*, the Moon Goddess.

God of pleasure and of truth.
Where the roll of music thrilling
Breaks in rapture, love distilling
  On the heart of buoyant youth!
Let the hermit seek a pathway
  'Tween extremes of good and ill;
We prefer the exaltation
Of a phrenzied divination,
  Making mortal pulses thrill!
Haste ye virgins of Astarte,
  Bring libations to her grove;
Bring the timbrel and the viol,
Spurn the code of self-denial—
  Taste the ravishment of love!

ELIJAH. Is there not in the universe of God
A safe retreat from sin? What strains are these
That harshly mingle with the morning song
Of turtle, plover, curlew and the lark?
Can shouts of revelry disturb me here,
So far removed from haunts of wickedness?
Methought this solitude might be a home
Of pure and lofty thought—
Of near communion with eternal life;
But now I find myself as far from these
As when the priests of Zidon stung my ears
With shameful hymns in praise of Ashtoreth.
Alas! a desert cannot interpose
A barrier between us and our sins:
Nor can the interval of space or time
Remove the burden of a guilty heart.
Hear me, Oh, Lord of Hosts,—
Thou that dwellest between the cherubim,
Shine forth! Shew me Thy glory, if in th' act
This body of decay should be consumed!

[*A glory surrounds* ELIJAH, *and a voice:* "No man can see My glory and live!" *Then* AZRIEL, *a seraph, appears to* ELIJAH *out of the glory that surrounds himself.*

c

ELIJAH. New lighted Wonder! What do I behold?
Another Tempter, clothed in light?
Ah, no! It cannot be that evil lurks
Behind the glory of this Presence!

AZRIEL. Fear not, Elijah; faithful Gileadite!
Fear not the presence of thy **Strength** and **Guide**.
Though all alone in this dread solitude,
The ever-wakeful Eye of God has o'er thee **watched**
With boundless love; while angels looked with **joy**
Upon a scene sublime as it is rare,—
A man of Sorrows, yet in Virtue armed,
Confronting all the evil of his age,
With soul erect!—a beacon to mankind!
Then steer right onward on thy noble course,
And I, who am thy fellow worshipper,
Will shield thee from ill fate.

ELIJAH. So many voices
Have lately fallen on mine ears perplexed,
That I am tossed about, like desert sands,
By every wind that blows,—weak in resolve,
In action fruitless, but in sorrow schooled!
Erewhile I heard a voice—
"Elijah, get thee hence,
At Cherith hide thyself;
Its waters shalt thou drink,
And Couriers of the air shall food provide."
But lo, the brook no more supplies
Its cooling draught;
Nor do the friendly birds,
At evening and at morning tide,
Remember if Elijah lives or no.
Alas! I am alone,
With burning zeal consumed,—
A warning monument of work undone,—
I gaze on Desolation!
Ah, why should Virtue, so divinely formed,
So loved of Heaven, be left unarmed on Earth,
And heir to so much sorrow and unrest—

Of heavy thoughts and watches of the night?
But who art thou, so fair in form and speech?

AZRIEL. My name is Azriel—the Fire of God;
And with this sword which once o'er Eden flamed,
Fast by the branches of the Tree of Life,
I touch thy hairy mantle, now transfigured;
Wrapt in its folds thou mayst confront the world!
For none can take thy life till I receive
Thee hence! Go forth, and to Zarepta turn;
Declare the coming of the Lord of Hosts,
To light the altars of his saints with fire!
Farewell, Elijah; we shall meet again,
When thou shalt know the mission of thy life! *

[AZRIEL *disappears, and* ELIJAH *is left once more alone.*

ELIJAH. "My name is Azriel—the Fire of God!"
Am I deceived by morning's sovereign light?
Or is't a vision of the inward eye,
Now purified in that celestial flame,
Which shone around the son of Amram's face
When from the mount he brought the Law of God?
O, Sacred Flame—divinest element!
Who feels thy presence shall remain unmoved
In storms of life as in the hour of death!
Let Tammuz and his wailing prophets howl
Their dire enchantments in Zarepta's groves,
Yet thither will I bend my course,
And prophesy the coming of the Lord of Hosts!

(*Chorus of* ANGELS *as the sun rises above the horizon.*)

1st ANGEL.   Hover around him,
    Ye angels of light;
  Bright visions of beauty
    Arise on his sight!

---

* This was at Horeb, when Elijah was sent to anoint kings and consecrate priests.

2nd Angel.   Zarepta of Zidon,
         Thy freedom is nigh,
      For the beacon of Carmel
         Is lighted on high;
      The prophets of Baal
         Are loud in their plain,
      And the priests of Astarte
         Invoke her in vain!

3rd Angel.   Seraphim, Cherubim,
      Wake your harps; welcome him—
   Welcome the faithful to God and mankind;
         Lo the brave Gileadite
         Comes in Jehovah's might,
      Mighty to scatter his foes to the wind!

             Chorus.
      Then will the hills rejoice,
      When in harmonious voice
   Angels and Shepherds unite in the song;—
         Trumpets of War shall cease,
         Princes shall reign in peace,—
   Love shall prevail o'er oppression and wrong!
         Then hover around him
            Ye Angels of Light!
            Ye Visions of Beauty
            Arise on his sight!
      And on his ear let heavenly music steal
         In melting strains of ravishing delight,
      That sight and sound may to his soul reveal
         The crowning Victory on Carmel height,
      When in the blaze of His ethereal Fire
         The Angel of the Lord shall quite o'erthrow
      The pomp of Ahab and the pride of Tyre
         With many a loud lament and lasting Woe!
         So shall the hills and groves
            No more resound
         With shouts of revelry and guilty loves*

   * These and similar expressions have reference to the licentious rites
in the worship of Astarte.

> Within the bound
> Of Judah's Heritage;
> But songs to the Most High
> Shall ring through earth and sky
> From lips of tender babe and hoary age!
> Then welcome him with song,
> Who in his God is strong,
> To live a hermit as to wear a crown!
> Hail, prophet of th' Invisible, all hail!
> Thy coming sheds a glory on the earth;
> The shadows flee, the powers of darkness quail,
> And guilty revels tremble in their birth.

END OF ACT I.

ACT II.—ELIJAH AT CARMEL.

SCENE I.

A Plain near Jezreel, at the foot of Carmel.

Enter AHAB, *who sees* ELIJAH *advancing towards him.*

AHAB. I know him by his visage and his garb,
His hairy mantle and his fierce aspect
Rebellious spirit! proud conspirator!—
What brow!—what eye!—black thunder wreathed in fire!
If overhanging clouds and forkèd light
Prognosticate a storm, methinks, indeed,
Another tempest speaks in this man's face;
Yet will I speak to him though he do shake
The solid earth with his accursèd tongue!

Enter ELIJAH.

Art thou the man that troubleth Israël
With thy magician tricks, and incantations?

ELIJAH. Not I, O King; but thou and Omri's house,
In that ye have forsaken Righteousness,
And gone a whoring after Ashtoreth!

AHAB. False phrophet! dost thou not regard thy life
In this mad phrenzy of heretic thought?

Renounce thy blasphemous and barborous creed,
Or, by my father's soul, thou diest!

ELIJAH. Have I so long endured without recoil,
And in the solitude of barren wastes,
The dread assaults of Satan and his host,—
And shall I now, in terror of thy name,
Abjure the Strength of Israël? Vain boaster!
My armour is intrenchant to thy sword—
Impervious to thy spear! The King of Kings,
Who sent me unto thee, hath spoken thus:
"Go, shew thyself to Ahab, and once more
Restore him in the Spirit of My love;
If he repent and harden not his heart,
In blind security, against the Truth,
Then will the rain descend in gracious showers,
The barren fields will yet again rejoice,
And fruitful harvests shall reward the toil
Of husbandry."

AHAB. Thou other Balaam's ass!
Prating of visions in thy stubborn will
To be rebellious! Has it come to this,
That, flattered by our royal clemency,
Thy proud, unmitigated vanity
Doth self-appoint thee censor of our reign?
Ha! dost thou lecture me on policy
And high affairs of state beyond thy ken,—
Yea, on religion! with "Thus saith the Lord!"
What Lord? Perchance the golden calf of Bethel,
Or he of Eckron, known as god of flies!
Go to; the God of Israël is Light,*
In whom there is no variableness!
And by His light I swear that thou shalt die!

ELIJAH. The God of Israël is Light, indeed,
But thou art left in utter darkness still.
Then hear thou this, ill-fated man,—
Since Mercy pleads in vain,

---

* Ahab means *Baal*, or the Sun god; but he unconsciously speaks the truth.

And hides her face in sorrow for thy sin,
A sterner Angel speaks,
And trumpet sounds in thy unwilling ear
The doom that shall await thy house,
If, in the revelation of that Light,
Thou reckest not its glory, and repent!
I challenge thee, with thy Zidonian priests,
In all the pomp and circumstance of state,
To meet me, in the name of that you serve,
On Carmel's airy top; there to dispute
With me alone the sovereignty of Truth!
Since thy appeal is to that element *
Which now consumes the earth, and brings
Lean famine unto every door,—
Prepare a sacrifice on yonder hill,
One for the priests of Baal, one for me;
And let the God who answers in the Fire
In which you trust,—let Him be God in Israël!

AHAB. O, vanity! Oh! ill-assorted pride!
How long shalt thou thy brazen trumpet blow,
And summon kings to parley with the mob?
Have I not said, Elijah, thou art mad—
A visionary dreamer of the type
Of Balaam, or of her of Endor old,
Whom God confounded in their blasphemy,
As eke he did the crownèd heads
Who trusted in their magic and their charms?
Thy soul, in common with the Gileadites,
Is, as the forest of the mountain side,
Rude, rugged, wild, luxuriant, rank,
For lack of culture and of gentle breeding;
And so it is that thy strange life is spent
In doing battle with thy gloomy thoughts—
Those dark and stormy passions of thy soul,—
Mistaking them for heavenly oracles,
As fancy dictates or self-love approves.

ELIJAH. Alas, my country! once the favoured home

* Namely, to the Sun or Baal.

Of patriarch fathers and of pious sons;
What evil scourge at length usurps thy throne,
And lights thy holy places with strange fire!
What thinkest thou—vain, weak and violent,
Fell persecutor of the saints of God?
Shall He, who smote the Gentiles with the sword
Of Gideon, but for idolatry,—
Shall He in Ahab love what He abhorred
In Midian? I tell thee, nay!
The sceptred Angel that descended then
To consecrate a soldier-priest,
The stout king-conquering Abieezerite,
Returns again in Ahab's cultured reign
To damn the counsels of his learnèd priests
And strip the court of Jezebel of all its gloss!

AHAB. Thou traitor knave! wouldst thou blaspheme the King?

ELIJAH. I own no King but One, whom thou deniest!

AHAB. Go, hide in caves or clefts of desert rocks
With lions, wolves and bears, and birds of night;
Thou art not fit to live in civil state,
Or hold communion with the gentle bred;
For ruin ever marks thy path, and blights
The lives of those that deign to give thee shelter!
Go to! Wouldst thou destroy, rebuild, reform
The faith and ritual of our ancestors?
Who gave Elijah this authority?
Who taught *him* wisdom since our fathers slept,
Or made him censor of the human race?
Art thou so boastful in comparisons
As overpeer the wisest man that lived—
The Son of David, who first taught in Zion
The worship of our goddess Ashtoreth?

ELIJAH. A precedent for sin is easy found,
As well upon the throne as in the hut!
The Son of David did as thou hast said,
And therefore was his kingdom rent in twain,
A prey to civil broils and base usurpers—
As witness Omri's house, and Jezebel!

AHAB. Ha! sayest thou? Then die, false traitor, die!

    [*The* KING *draws his sword, but is paralysed by the
    majesty of* ELIJAH'S *presence.*

Nay, nay; I will be guiltless of thy death,
Nor will I soil my blade with blood of thine.
Thou art unarmed; and Ahab's sword is made
To shield, not smite, defenceless heads!

ELIJAH.   Unarmed!
I fear no weapon that a King can wield!
I fear for thee, O man, whom God hath raised,
In virtue of thy many noble gifts,
Unto the highest top of sovereignty,—
That dallying with the evil of thy court
Thou hast become the helpless slave of sin,
Entwined within the folds of female charms,
Enchanted by the sparkle of her cup,
Till thou hast quite forgot thy sacred trust,
In the mad whirl of pleasure's giddy round!
Who can deliver thee from these same toils
With which the goddess, Pleasure, fetters thee,
But Him who taught our fathers from of old,
That sin in every form, however glossed,
Is the grand parent of our misery!
Thou art not happy, man —Ah, no!
The heartache and remorse; the bitter pangs
That mock relief—that brood of sin begot—
Have made thee what thou art—their helpless prey!
Hast thou forgot those other days,
When in the glory of thy golden prime,
Thy youth gave promise of a nobler growth
Than that which now disgraces all thy reign?—
The Law of God despised—
His altars overthrown—His prophets slain—
And our beloved country scourged
By mercenary hirelings of thy court?
Compare the promise then with its fruition now,
And say, Where is the peace and rest,—
Where is the King that reigneth righteously,

The father of his people, and their shield
Against oppression, tyranny and wrong!

AHAB. No more! for thou hast touched a mortal wound
That rankles in my breast! Say rather this,—
Why am I a King; and thou, with all thy faith,
Art but a wandering waif—a castaway!

ELIJAH. Yet would I not exchange my state of mind,
Pent as it is in want and poverty,
For purple robes, with regal misery.

AHAB. More pride is hid beneath that hairy cloak,
And in the guise of lowliness of heart,
Than swells the bosom of a conqueror!
Yet, though I neither reverence gods nor priests,
Nor such as ape the seeing of the prophet,
I will accept thy challenge; and at noon,
Before the sun has bent his downward course
From his meridian blaze, I will confront
My faith with thine on Carmel's skyey top!

ELIJAH. So let the God, who answereth by Fire,
Be evermore the Strength of Israël!

AHAB. Farewell. We meet to make thy vaunting true!

[*Exeunt.*

ANGELIC CHORUS.

Who taught Elijah heavenly things
  When priests were all in error lost?
Who taught him pilotage when Kings
  Were tempest-tossed?
Who taught the sun to shine
  And flowers to spring?
The energy Divine,
  Whereof the angels sing!
'Twas sorrow forged within his soul,
  The thoughts that strike like polished shafts,
And purged his heart of sin, and dole
  With bitter draughts!
Sad nurse of pure and lofty thought;
  Stern priestess of the mysteries!

Thou hast the gates of knowledge wrought,
    And hold'st the keys!
        With God he wrestled and prevailed
            In watches of the silent night;
        When all the world its pleasure hailed,
            He hailed the Light!
Hail, trumpet-tongued, Almighty Thunderer!
    Thine is the Fire of God, the Fire to blast
The foes of Ancient Truth, and sunder her
    From the vile dross in which she has been cast
In age of big Despair and Darkness vast!
    Hail, great Recluse!
The prophet, patriot, met in one!
    Behold the sluice
Of his deep soul is opened, and the throne
Of Ahab shakes before that mighty flood alone!

SCENE II.

Top of Carmel. ELIJAH *standing alone by the side of a broken altar.*

ELIJAH. These stones, though mute, bear witness to a faith
    That made the name of Israel glorious,
    And Judah's land a heritage of saints.
    Sad records of the past!—Dumb monuments
    Of ancient Piety!—alas, how changed!
    Here stood the altars of the Living God,
    And here His prophets stood, fire-sanctified,
    To teach His people holiness of life,
    Through the atoning grace of sacrifice!
    But now the Baal worship of Jezreel,
    The calf idolatry of Samaria,
    And the licentious rites of Ashtoreth—
    That amorous goddess of the Tyrians—
    Usurp our Holy Places, and corrupt

The springs of virtue and the wells of life.
My spirit burns to see that Faith restored,
Which led the son of Amram to renounce
The gods of Egypt and their hateful shrines
For the Eternal Majesty of Heaven;
Whose temple is the naked firmament,
Whose altars are the Sinai's of the world,
Reared by His own Almighty Hand,
And lit in flames all glorious as His Presence!
Return, O Lord! —how long shall error triumph?
How long shall Kings exalt Iniquity,
And Queens respect the vile and profligate,
While Virtue blushes, and retires from scenes
That make the Earth belie its origin!
Unhappy Mother of the human race!—
Who can deliver thee from Satan's wiles
And cleanse thy blood-stained bosom from the guilt
Of thine own offspring? Must another flood
In terror, but in mercy cover thee?
The Faithful and the Just who cannot err
Hath said, He will not visit thee again
In judgment from the fountains of the Deep;
But there is Fire in Heaven!—that Element
Reserved in God's Right Hand to blast the growth
Of such disease and moral leprosy
As smote the Cities of the Plain with death!

(*An evil spirit, in the shape of a Raven, perches on a rock close to* ELIJAH.)

RAVEN.   In this hubbub of religion,
            What is false or what is true?
         Priests arrayed against each other—
            Nothing strange and nothing new!
         "This is god," says one poor devil;
            "This is he," another cries;
         And what this one deems most sacred,
            That one mocks, denies, defies!
         What a hubbub, friend Elijah,
            All about an empty word!—

Baal, Ashtoreth, Jehovah!—
　　Is it Reptile, Fish, or Bird?
Tell us, for we have no college,
　　Why you differ, men of God!
Why not learn a universal
　　Language, like our croak and nod!

ELIJAH. O bird accursed! since Noah sent thee forth!—
Thou ever faithless, never to be trusted,—
Thou, in the craving of thy filthy maw,
Forgot'st thy better mission and did'st gorge
Thyself on carrion on some death-ridden shore!
So shalt thou be a bird of evil omen
Unto all time!

RAVEN (*flying away*). Croak! It was not so at Cherith,
　　When the ravens brought thee food;
Then thou did'st not call it carrion,
　　But esteemed it passing good!
Still deserted, still forsaken,
　　May thou ever live apart!
World-defying, life-despairing,
　　With the vulture at thine heart!

(*A good Spirit in the shape of a Dove now perches on the broken altar.*)

DOVE.　　　　Be strong in faith,
　　　　　　And waver not,
　　　　　　Though doubt and fear
　　　　　　　Alternate blot,
　　　　　　With shadows dark,
　　　　　　　The Light Above,
　　　　　　And quench the fire
　　　　　　　Of hope and love!
　　　　　　The clouds of doubt
　　　　　　　Shall pass away
　　　　　　As shadows flee
　　　　　　　Before the day;
　　　　　　And hope and love
　　　　　　　Will spring to light

When steadfast faith
  Sustains the fight!
Be strong in Faith,—
  Sustain the shock
Of this assault
  Firm as a rock!
When tempests roar
  And clouds are driven
Along the vault
  Of angry heaven,
The seated hills
  Unshaken stand
Till Light returns
  At God's command.
The darkest hour
  Precedes the dawn,
And honey sweet
  From bitter herbs is drawn!

ELIJAH. Dear bird of promise, love and peace!
  Emblem of Humility,
  And of her sister, Charity!
Let not that song of thine for ever cease!
It strikes responsive chords within my breast,
  Unused to lighter strains,
  Than such as still the ear of Faith retains,
In this sad life of warfare and unrest!
And there thou sittest, gentle, meek, and pure,
  Where once the glory of the Lord did shine,—
  As if the burden of my sins were thine,
And thou wert willing to endure
The anguish of atoning Love
  In yielding up thy breath,
  And with thy death,
New-reconcile me to my God above!

DOVE.   Be strong in faith,
    Sustain the shock
  Of evil doubt
    Firm as a rock!

The time shall come,
  The world shall hear
My Voice proclaim
  In accents clear—
" This is My Son,
  " O, hear His Voice;
" Ye weary hearts
  " In Him rejoice!"
Then Kings shall reign
  In virtues mild,
Taught in the world
  By God's own Child!
Who shall be called
  The Prince of Peace,
For in His Love
  Grim War shall cease.
Be strong in faith,
  Sustain the shock
Of evil doubt
  Firm as a Rock!

[*The* DOVE *flies away.*

ELIJAH. That time shall come; but now 'tis force prevails,
  And violence drives on her car triumphant!
  The world is dark, and filled with deeds too foul
  And horrible to be recorded!—
  But welcome, brood of Hell! confront me here!
  Already have I conquered one by one,
  Within this little Kingdom of myself,
  Your direst chiefs—Lust, Luxury, and Pride!
  Now come in your battalions—show your ranks,
  Led by your votaries, the priests of Baal,
  And in the livery of his faith bedight
  Display at once your rage and impotence,—
  Your fury baffled, and your magic foiled!

  (*Seeing* AHAB *and his Train advancing.*)

  Here comes the King of Israel—deaf and blind
  As are his own idols! O, man misled
  By the bright sparkle of that fatal charm—

The fascination of a woman's eye!
And the lascivious ceremonial
Of temples dedicated to the Shame—
The Curse and Shame of Israël!
What will thy hollow forms avail thee now
When the Great Searcher of the hearts of men
Descends in withering blasts of fire
Amidst the chaff and stubble of thy Court?
Unseal his eyes, O Thou All-Seeing One,
That he may see Thy Glory, and return
From error's devious path and mortal end
To that which leads the soul to truth and light!
In this dread hour of conflict with the Prince
Of Darkness, fraught with issues that will shape
The course of history for future time;
In this divine unfolding of Thyself,
Preserve the life of Ahab from ill fate!
He may repent, for he has known the truth;
But as for them, these priestlings of his house,
Let none escape—scatter their ashes to the winds!

Enter AHAB, PRIESTS *and Chorus of Elders.*

CHORUS.

On and on throughout the ages,
    Ever learning, never knowing,
Man but fills historic pages
    With his errors, ever growing!
Wearied, baffled and contending,
    He is worn with toil and grief,
In ascending
    Altar stairs of false belief!
Who can shew him any good,
    Heart-renewing, sorrow-healing,
Or restore the light of youth,
    All around him God revealing?
As the glory of the East
    At the rising of the sun,
So the glory of the West
    When his daily course is run.

Thus in humility
    Old age resumes the heavenly garb of youth—
    Its glory, radiancy, and simple truth!
Till clad in mystic light of calm tranquility,
    It disappears from mortal view
Into the mansions of the saints at rest,
    And mantled in the hue,
With which the morning of its life was blest!
Ah, happy youth! fresh as the budding rose
    In the first blush of the ascending light!
What dreams are thine, prophetic of repose,—
    Of life to come—a paradise of dear delight!
As if the world contained
Primeval life unstained,
    With all the glory of the bridal morn,
When first the wedded pair
In Eden stood as fair
    As the untainted source whence they were born!
But ah, the withering heat of noon
    Dried up the morning dew
    And lent another hue
To youth's career, alas, too soon!
The blasting furnace of the daily strife,
    Did shrivel up the blossom without ruth;
    And what remained of youth
Was but the dream of some far distant life!
Ah, where is now the heavenly rest,
    The promise of the vision and the dream;
    Is every hope eclipsed and not a gleam
To nurse immortal thought within the breast?
    Ah, who can shew him any good,
    Within his awful solitude
Of doubt and care?
    Where sin and sorrow reign in state,
    And Pleasure leads but to the Gate
Of dark Despair!
    For Sin will darken life,
    And shew it but a wilderness of strife;
Where living waters never flow,
And fragrant flowers never grow,

   Or wear a bloom!
 Man still pursues some phantom bliss,
 And still his journey ends in this—
   To find a tomb!
 His pilgrimage is but a dream
   Of something future or of something past—
 The memory of things which once did seem,
   Or hope of things that never see the light,
 Until at last,
   He welcomes the repose of a good night,—
 And sinks into the grave to rise no more,—
 His soul is free, his dream of life is o'er!

ELIJAH. How long 'tween two opinions do ye halt?
  If Baal be the God, then follow him;
  But if the Lord be God, then follow Him!
    Is there no answer, none?
  Alas, poor sheep! have you forgot your fold?
  Have you so long been straying shepherdless,
  That you forget the voice, the very name,
  Of Him who led our fathers by the streams
  And pleasant pasturage of Judah's land?
  Look here!—have you forgot these altar stones,
  The Consecrated tokens of the Covenant
  Made to our Ancestor when he prevailed
  At Peniel? Have you indeed forgot
  The meaning of the name he then received,
  That like his brother Esau you despise
  Your heritage; and for the idols of the land,
  Forsake the Shepherd and the Strength of Israel?
  Behold these prophets of the Baalim—
  A goodly multitude!—and I alone,
  The only prophet of the Living God,
  Opposing challenge them! Here let us build
  Two altars, one for God, and one for Baal!
  Let him be God this day in Israel
  Who shews his glory in a flame of fire,
  Upon the altar of His covenant!

(*The altars are being built and the Chorus of* ELDERS *reply.*)

Chorus.

'Tis well, 'tis well,
  O prophet bold!
  That sacred Fire of old,
Will doubt and dispute quell!
Let Him be God indeed,
  Who thus reveals his glory,
And scatter error's seed
  As erst in ancient story,
When that rebellious crew
  Of Korah challenged God and Truth;
  Full soon they learnt in bitter ruth
The Power of Him the faithful Prophet* knew.
Again let Israel see
  The Glory of their God;
Again their enemy
  Shall kiss the rod!
A nameless fear
  Now chills the faithless heart,
And whispers in the ear
  The terror of His nod
Which makes the mountains start!—
  The terror of His thunder,
At which the Earth and Ocean,
In dread commotion,
  Reel back amazed
  Before His fiery arm upraised,
To smite the tyrants of the world asunder!
  Then tremble ye who would adore
Your idol gods of wood and stone,
And worship Him alone
  Who made the ancient heavens, and the Moun-
                                    [tains hoar!

(*The altars are now prepared and the Sacrifices laid upon them.*
The Priests *of* Baal *approach one of the altars and invoke their God*).

* Moses.

PRIESTS OF BAAL. O, Baal, hear,
　　Bow down thine ear
　　And hearken to our prayers as we cry!
　　Dismiss thine arrows keen,
　　Winged with the flashing sheen
　　Of thine eternal orb ensphered on high!
　　O, Baal, hear,
　　Bow down thine ear,
　　Thou god for whom a thousand Victims die!
　　Thou cloud-compelling god of light,
　　Thine altar is with Sacrifice bedight,
　　And waits the flaming brand
　　Of thy destroying hand
　　To touch it as thy glory passeth by!

ELIJAH. Ha! cry aloud and rouse this sluggard god,
　　Who is perchance asleep and must be waked!
　　Or peradventure he may be from home,
　　On some affair of pleasure or of state;
　　But he's a god! and surely he can hear
　　The lusty cries of some four hundred priests!
　　Then cry again, and louder than before;
　　Mayhap he takes his noon siesta now
　　And must be roused by louder cries and knocks!

PRIESTS. O, Baal, hear!—
　　Thou Scatterer of darkness and of night!—
　　And from thy highest sphere
　　Of pure unutterable light,
　　Send forth thy shaft with fiery speed,
　　Thou dreaded god, for whom our bodies bleed!
　　Behold this sacrifice
　　With which we mingle human blood;—
　　Let it suffice,
　　O God of fire
　　To pacify thine ire,
　　And quench it in this crimson flood!

ELIJAH. Behold these baffled worshippers of Baal!—
　　Self-tortured, yet forsaken by their god!
　　Self-sacrificed, yet Baal recketh not!
　　Such is the fashion of their sensuous creed!

But now draw near to me, and once again
Stand by the Altar of the True and Just!
When ye shall see the angel of the lord,
In all the glory of His Majesty,
Descend in the Shekinah long departed
From the forsaken shrines of Israel!

ELDERS. 'Tis well, 'tis well,
    O prophet bold!
    That sacred Fire of old
    Will doubt and error quell! &c.

ELIJAH. Lord, God of Abram, Isaac, and of Israel!
Let it be known this day that thou art God;
And I, thy Servant, hath obeyed thy voice,
And done all this at thy command. Hear me!
O Lord, my God, hear me! not for my sake,
But for thy people's sake, that they may know
THOU ART! thou only the Allseeing One!
So shall their hearts be turned to thee again,
Thou strength of heart.—Almighty Love!

(AZRIEL *descends in a flame of fire on* ELIJAH'S *Altar and lights the sacrifice*).

AZRIEL. In Sacrificial fire,
    And Self-denying flame
  Of all-atoning LOVE,
  I come from Heaven above!
    And in JEHOVAH'S name,
  I burn, consume, devour,
  The shame, the guilt, the power
    Of SIN upon this consecrated Pyre!
  I am the first creation of His voice,
    Since from of old It cried, 'Let there be Light!'
    I still remain untainted in His sight,
    And in His Law rejoice—
      Appearing thus in Mercy or in Ire,
  To blast the grovelling soul, the lofty to inspire!

(*The Sacrifice is consumed to ashes, and the Chorus of* ELDERS *rejoice.*)

Chorus of Elders.

O ye tumultuous hearts, break forth in Song!—
  The Lord is God!
Let Heaven and Earth the great refrain prolong,—
  The Lord is God!
He said of old, 'Let there be Light!'
  Primeval Chaos heard the sound
  Of that almighty tone,
  And started from his throne
In sudden fright,
  To see the new created beam
Flash through the realms of Night!
  Then Darkness fled apace,
  Before the Glory of His face;
And all around
The depths profound
  Of vast illimitable space,
The starry spheres did chime
The dawning hour and golden birth of Time!
  The mighty diapason then began,
The angels choiring to the orbs above;
  The spark divine awaked the song in man,
And all was harmony and love!
  But Oh, the discord destined to prevail
When Woman's* counsel ruled his fate;
  The song of triumph changed to bitter wail,—
Pure innocence and love to guilt and hate!
    O Light divine,
    Upon us shine,
  Break through the chaos of the mind!
    Truth Revealer,
    Sorrow Healer
  Restore their seeing to the blind.
    Redeem the lost,
    By error tossed,
  Upon the Stormy sea of life!
    And with the Word

---

*Directly, Eve; *indirectly*, Jezebel.

    Through Chaos heard
     Compose the discord and the Strife!
  The Lord is God! where are your idols now?
    Ye priests of Baal and the Tyrian Queen!
  Unhallowed are the shrines before you bow,
    And fireless are your altars and unclean
  That sacrifice of shame
  You offer in the name
    Of him who made the son of Nebat fall
  Into the lowest deep of sin,
  And with his idols win
    The heart of Israel from the Lord of all!

ELIJAH. What sayest thou, O King! Dost thou believe
  In thy grim idol still? Hast thou not seen
  Such things as might inspire thy soul with awe,
  And render faith as natural as sight?

AHAB. O, mighty prophet of the Living God,
  Thou true and faithful counsellor!
  Thy words to me are terrible
  As the sharp edgèd levin fire
  That has devoured thy sacrifice!
  I now believe in very deed
  That thou alone art worthy to be called
  The prophet and the priest of the Most High.

ELIJAH. God speaks in love, and man regards Him not;
  He speaks in terror, then revives the sin
  So long forgot! Trust not the easy faith
  Which walks by light, and stumbles in the dark;
  But lean on virtues which can flourish best,
  Not in the calms but in the storms of life!
  'Tis not for lack of knowledge but of love
  That thou hast failed! The light may point the way,
  But love alone can make for righteousness!

AHAB. Most true! My heart misled by lying priests,
  Has only known the pain of passion,
  The grief of hate and the deceit of sense—
  Yea, all such things as starve the soul

E'en in the act of feasting on their honey!
And thus it is my life is one disease
Since I have sought my ills by ills to cure!
But if thou wouldst restore my peace of mind,
And re-establish faith upon her throne,
Shew me the living streams that quench all thirst,
And leave no haunting shadow to torment
The soul that drinks them to satiety!
Teach me the love that makes for Righteousness,
And I will cherish it for evermore!

ELIJAH. Love well thy country, and thy people well;
  For he can love the Lord of Heaven best
  Who first has learnt to love all living souls.
  Labour and love—deny thyself and live!
  So shalt thou learn the bliss of self-control;
  Destroy thine idols and those lying priests,
  And cleave thee to the Strength of Israel;
  So shalt thou open up a path to peace
  And win the glory born of suffering!

AHAB. What, must we slay all Baal's priests?

ELIJAH Destroy them all—let none of them escape,
  Lest they again should lead thy heart astray.
  For as in marshes where diseases lurk,
  Pale glimmering lights allure night-foundered men,
  So when the constitution of a State
  Is rot, more priests are bred! Then throughly purge
  The body politic of their infection;
  And let the guides who led thee into shame
  Be put to death—aye, root and branch!

AHAB. And yet I am to love all living souls!

ELIJAH. Ah, thou art falling into questionings,
  Inspired by evil spirits of the Deep!
  Beware, lest when God speaks to thee again
  His Justice visit thee as now His Grace,
  And wither thee as with a blast of fire!
  The Lord hath said, Destroy the priests of Baal!
  And in obedience lies thy only hope.
  If thou art wise, seek not to know too much;

> For by such arts the Devil oft prevails,
> And damns the spirit which he most informs!
> Learn that which profiteth; but leave the rest
> To Him who orders all things for the best!

AHAB. Then let the clarions and the trumpets sound
> The triumph of Elijah, and the knell
> Of these four hundred dreamers* of the Bel!

(The Priests are led to execution.)

PRIESTS. Alas, I am undone,
> The haunting shadows hover nigh!
> Farewell, thou glorious Sun,
> In thee I trusted and in thee I die!
> Ah, cruel fate!
> To be for ever banished from thy beam,
> To wed corruption, and with worms to mate,
> To sleep with Horror and of Hell to dream!
> Ah, why not leave me to forego
> This life in peace!
> Then should I never dread
> The mansions of the dead,
> But hail the soul's release
> From this distracted frame o'erwrought with woe!
> Farewell, thou God of light,
> No more shall incense from thine altars rise;
> In vain I worshipped in thy sight,
> In vain my prayers pierced the skies;
> Then welcome endless night and dreamless sleep,
> Nor gods nor prophets can disturb that slumber deep.

ELIJAH. The soul survives in torment or in bliss
> As we have pillowed it on earthly hopes
> Or on the Bosom of the Infinite!

AHAB. Away with them— the lying, juggling knaves!

(After the PRIESTS *are put to death a chorus of* ELDERS *follows)*

* DEUTERONOMY xiii.

Chorus of Elders.

Eternal Justice stands
Between the endless jar of right and wrong,
  And with impartial hands
Deals forth the merits which to life belong.
  She winnows with her fan
The harvest of our sowing;
  And on the treasures of the heart of man
She turns the purging blast for ever blowing!
  The chaff is blown away,
And scattered in the tempest of her breath;
  So perish all the wicked in the day
Jehovah sends His messenger of death!
  Ah, woe to them who work iniquity,
And feel no holy awe
  Or reverence for the majesty
And might of ancient Law!
  To them the grave is but the gate of Hell,
Where dreams of diverse horrors ever wake!
  Open ye gates, and let the priests of Bel
Pass to the torments of the fiery Lake!
  Is death the goal of life—
The silence deep
  Where end the heartache and the strife
In endless sleep?
  Ah, no! The grave is but the resting place
Of weary men,
  Where they lay down
The burden of accumulating years
  To rise again,
Delivered from their tears,
  To shine before Jehovah's face,
Immortal as the light that flashes in His crown!

Elijah. Does God require a sacerdotal caste,
  A priestly armament to fence the Truth?
Behold this heritage of death—
This mangled heap, this Baal sacrifice
To pride, ambition, vanity and lies!
Then say what is the pageantry of Courts,

> The gloss of ritual, and the pomp of priests,
> Confronted with the majesty of Heaven?

AHAB. Yea, I have erred and played the fool exceedingly!
> What yet remains that I should do?

ELIJAH.   Repent—repent!
> For godly sorrow is the nurse of joy,
> And woe is oft the guide to Heavenly Light!
> Dismiss the prophets of the grove, now fed
> By Jezebel; thus having purged thy Court,
> Restore the worship of the Lord thy God,
> Which Zion knew ere yet her glory fled.

AHAB. Amen! And thou shalt be my counsellor
> To lead me in the path of truth and light!

ELIJAH. May God, the Strength of Israel, be thy Guide!
> But now arise and haste thee to Jezreel;
> For lo! the heavens are darkening, and the sound
> Of rain abundant warns thee to make haste!

CHORUS OF ELDERS.

The heavens are darkening! the resounding shore
 Is white and sparkling with the snowy spray!
The billows swell to mountains, and leap o'er
 Their rocky barrier in their awful play!
The noble barque which carries home the brave
Is but a toy on yonder crested wave!
The darkness deepens, and the clouds
 Are rent asunder by the rushing winds;
The Sun is buried in his shrouds,
 And from their fringes drop the rain,
 On mountain, valley and on plain;
As weeping o'er the thirsty ground
With pity and with love profound,
Bedewing it with heavenly tears,—
As doth a mother when she fears
The fever that afflicts her child
Should wither all her hope, and be by death beguiled.
The sky with sea is blent,
The clouds, with thunder rent,

Echo the clamour of the bellowing shore!
   The billows swelling high
   Rise to salute the sky,—
Unite their loud voices to the deafening roar!
   The fiery javelin's leap
   From deep to deep!
Hurled by an Arm resistless in its might!
   They speed on wings of flame,
   Swifter than we exclaim!
And vanish in the bosom of the night!
   Dark, wild and clamorous,
   Hot, fierce and amorous,
The heavens embrace the earth rejoicing as a bride!
   With her new garments on,
   Her fasting days are gone,
And in the great embrace each pulse is vivified!
   See how the valleys smile
   As when the fruitful Nile
Scatters his living verdure all around;
   When springs to life the fruit,
   Ordained for man and brute,
As the reward of toil, with blessing crowned!
   Oh, mighty power of Prayer!—
   And Faith her sister fair,
Who held her arms uplifted to the sky!
   In steadfast loving trust
   In Him who made the dust
To yield its fruit, and in its season multiply!
   Rejoice, thou barren Earth! no more the tomb
Of cruel famine and of big despair;
   For thou shalt bear within thy teeming womb
The fruit of noble toil,—
The triumph and the spoil
   Of peaceful industry and happy care!
Rejoice, thou barren Earth! and bloom again,
   As thou wert wont ere Sin had marred thy face!
Ere Tyranny enthroned began to reign,
And Famine lean and bloody War
Were yoked together in his car,
   To mock at God and curse the human race!

Enwreathed in clouds of incense smelling sweet,
Enveloped in a flame of heavenly love,
The prophet of Jehovah comes to greet
The offspring of his zeal—
The freedom and the commonweal
Of Israël on earth, as of the saints above.

END OF ACT II.

ACT III.—ELIJAH AT HOREB.

(Forty days after the Scene on Carmel.)

SCENE I.

(The Priests of ASTARTE *carousing in their Hall in the Palace of* AHAB *at Jezreel.)*

Enter TAMAL, ISATOL, *and* SINADAB *Priests.*

TAMAL. What ails our lord, the King, that he foregoes
    His wonted pleasures and his merrymakings?
    I should not wonder if he took to caves,
    And doffed his royal robes for hairy skins!
SINADAB. And like another Saul, be found among
    The prophets!—ha, ha!
ISHTOL.   Or like a Solomon,
    Return to wisdom, madness, and to folly!
SINADAB. Or take to scratching doors as David did,
    And let his spittle fall adown his beard!
TAMAL. The gods are just, and madness* is the curse
    With which they smite the disobedient!
    E'en since that day he was prevailed upon
    To slay our holy brethren in the sight
    Of their own altar, Ahab has been mad!
ISHTOL. He might have slain us too, or banished us
    To Zidon, save for Jezebel, our Queen.
    That Wizard Gileadite has shook his faith

---

* Deut. xxviii: 28

                    In our most sacred rites; and even now
                    We are not safe—his madness is so plain!
SINADAB. The fairest Jezebel will exorcise
                    Her lord! She will provide some other blood
                    To dull the appetite and calm the rage
                    Of this mankilling tiger of a King!
TAMAL. I hope Elijah will the Victim be!—
SINADAB. His blood would seal a longer term of peace
                    Than that of all the Naboths of Jezreel!
TAMAL. And so 'tis true that Naboth is to hang!
SINADAB. 'Tis so decreed by our most gracious Queen,
                    Who wants her lord to cultivate the Vine,
                    And worship Bacchus, since he lost his Bel!
ALL. Ha, ha, ha, ha! Bacchus and Bel for ever!
ISHTOL. But how that wizard could have brought the rain
                    Is quite beyond my reckoning. 'Tis strange
                    His prayer was heard and answered by the gods!—
                    What say you, Sinadab—do you believe?
SINADAB. Believe in gods? Ha, ha! you know I do—
                    In gods and goddesses if they are fair!
                    But to be serious with you, brother mine;
                    The rain would have descended at the time,
                    The nimble stroke of lightning would have struck,
                    If such a man as he had never lived.
                    The arbitration of two rival gods—
                    A custom known to heathen worshippers—
                    Is but the juggling trick of arrant knaves!
ISHTOL. But then the Sacrifice, my Sinadab!—
                    Elijah's Sacrifice alone was struck!
SINADAB. In any thunderstorm on Carmel's Top,
                    I could perform a miracle as great!
                    'Tis known in Egypt and Phoenicia
                    That all metallic ores and substances
                    Have with the heavens a strange affinity;
                    The Magi, therefore, when they sacrifice,
                    Transfix their victim with sharp-pointed rods

Of polished brass; and as the thunderbolt
Shoots to the points where metals most abound,
The vulgar stare and cry, 'Behold a god!'

TAMAL. How should he know the storm was near?

SINADAB. How should he know? He is a Magician
And learnèd in the starry influences;
He keeps his vigils 'neath the naked sky,
And reads events in that mysterious scroll
Which is unfolded as the year revolves.

TAMAL. Starry influences! Why let us sing
Of other stars, and leave this to the devil,
Who certes knows more about it than we do!

ALL. Ha, ha, ha! The star of Zidon for ever!

SONG.

My love is like the Eastern Star,
  Bright herald angel of the morn,
Although her glances beam afar,
  Her heart from mine can ne'er be torn.

CHORUS.

I fill a cup with glowing wine,
  And pledge my love who lives afar;
Though other maids may be divine,
  I drink to her who lives afar!

Of all the Virgin Maids of Tyre
  She is the fairest Maid by far;
For her I tune the sounding lyre
  To sing of love for her afar!
No other love will shed its ray
  On me if not this love afar;
A brighter one where'r I stray,
  I shall not see or near or far;
My heart is glowing in a flame,
  And flashes love to her afar;
There is a rapture in the name
  Of her who is my morning star!

Ah gentle maiden list my lays,
   And smile upon me as a star!
Until the light of other days
   Shall break upon me from afar!

CHORUS.

Then fill your cups with glowing wine,
   And pledge my love who lives afar;
Though other maids may be divine,
   I drink to her who lives afar!

SINADAB. Go to! I'd sing you the length of a Sabbath day's journey in the same vein! Here's a specimen:—

O, Tammal man, if you are wise,
   Ah, never throw your mouth ajar,
To sing of love and starry eyes
   Where'er they be, or near or far!

But, hark! I hear the vesper trump! Then off we go, warm in the glow of vestal fires ascending!

[*Exeunt all, chanting.*

While this blood my body warms,
I will revel in their charms!
Rosy lips and loving arms
   Would make a priest divine, man!

SCENE II.

A Hall in the same.

Enter AHAB *alone.*

AHAB.* Life—death! To suffer and endure, is life!
And to be nothing, but—to be at rest,
Is death! Why love the life in which we fear,
And fear the everlasting truce
Which covers failure with oblivion;
Annuls the difference between defeats
And victories; levels the pyramids
Of noblest toil with the poor dust
From whence they sprang, and leave the great I AM,
Sole, self-existing Being as of old!
We *hope* our souls may live in some hereafter;—
That this poor lamp, when it has burnt to stench,
Will be re-kindled in a *better* world!
And what is hope? A beautiful illusion
That makes our little life a mockery—
The sport of fools, the laughter of the gods!
And yet, deluded still by this mirage,
We build a future life on present dreams!
How are my dreams of youth fulfilled?
Oh, God! how pure the world was then to me!
Earth, Air, and Ocean, all seemed newly made,
Still glowing with celestial radiancy,
As when on Eden the first morning smiled,
Effulgent in the glory
Of its great Origin and Fountain head!

---

* Tragic situations, says Goethe, spring from a conflict between "*the pretended freedom of the Will, and the necessary course of the* WHOLE." Ahab, having once violated an eternal law, seeks relief in criminal acts, each of which plunges him into "deeper consequences," until he becomes irredeemably lost in the *natural course of events.* Nevertheless, Ahab's original temptations were not, and could not be, so terrible as those which assailed Elijah; but the latter knew them from the first to be the "instruments of darkness," while the former yields to every evil impulse, and is miserable only in the *consequences* of his crimes. Therefore the paths of the King and the Prophet lead—the one to utter Darkness, and the other to Light Everlasting.

What are they now? The Earth a wilderness;
The Sea a melancholy waste; the Sky
A sheet of molten brass that scorches me!
Or is the dreary change within myself?
Into the joyless chasms of my soul
No light can penetrate! The sights and sounds
Of Nature, that were wont to elevate
My mind, and bathe it in the hues of heaven,
Are now one awful void—total eclipse!
My own dark shadow hides the face of things,
And I am in myself a living tomb;
What prophet to believe, what god to trust,
I know not. Ha! I've ceased to trust myself,
Or justify myself unto myself!
What then remains for Ahab but to rush
Headlong on fate, and challenge all the worst
That gods or devels can accumulate!
I shall forestall my destiny, and, like
Another Samson, perish in the wreck
Of all who dare oppoose my royal will!

Enter JEZEBEL.

Here comes the genius of my soul's desire!

JEZ. What demon bids thee thus to live apart,—
Draining the lees of melancholy thought,
And worshipping such spectres as arise
From the dead ashes of thy former fire?
Where now the princely spirit that would dare
Confront a world in arms and never quail?
Gone!—Blasted by a set of howling curs!

AHAB. 'Tis my own spectre, stained with guiltless blood,
That stands between me and my proper self!
I am not Ahab: there is incorporate
With me another spirit than my own,
Companioning my dreary solitude!

JEZ. The King of Israel is become a child,
And fears to walk alone in the dark!
What demon, ghost, or goblin frights him thus?

AHAB.　The shades of all the prophets we have slain
　　　　Are stronger in their unsubstantial horror
　　　　Than armèd legions clothed in flesh and blood!
　　　　And if this Tishbite should be caught at last,
　　　　And made a prisoner by our messengers,
　　　　I cannot lay a violent hand on him;—
　　　　I will be guiltless of *his* blood, at least.

JEZ.　　Has *he* not slain our prophets with the sword,
　　　　And caused a mutiny among our lieges,—
　　　　And shall we spare that man who caused us shame?
　　　　Oh, my eternal curse be upon the knave—
　　　　On all who would protect him from my fury!
　　　　Yes—blood by blood can only be atoned,
　　　　And nothing can atone for that day's work,—
　　　　Nothing will exorcise your soul possessed,
　　　　And cleanse your conscience of the stain,
　　　　Or reconcile you to th' immortal gods,
　　　　But the swift shedding of Elijah's blood!
　　　　Devils and darkness!—could I wield a sword,
　　　　His head had long ere this been food for ravens!
　　　　But hark! I hear the trumpet sound. 'Tis they!
　　　　　　　　　　　　　　　[*Sound of trumpets.*

AHAB (*aside*).　'Tis they, indeed! But how can I confront
　　　　This man whose eye doth paralyse my motion,
　　　　Rebukes my spirit, pride, and fell intent—
　　　　Scorches me like the eye of heaven itself!
　　　　How shall I answer for my conduct now?
　　　　What vain excuse, what sorry subterfuge
　　　　Can grace the front of disobedience,
　　　　Or nullify the revelation on the Mount?

　　　　　　Enter GUARDS *and* MESSENGER.

　　　　How now,—where is your prisoner?

MES.　　　　　　　　　　　　　　My lord,
　　　　If it may please your Majesty to hear,
　　　　For forty days we have been on the march,
　　　　And sleep has seldom closed our watchful eyes,
　　　　Since——

JEZ. Out! you slave, where is your prisoner?

MES. Most gracious queen! we searched the regions round,
The Valley of the Jordan to the Wilderness,—
Each cave and cavern, cot and Arab tent,—
We hunted up and down as for a prey;
But oft as we have been upon the trail
We failed to track the lion to his lair.

JEZ. You dare return alive to tell me this?
Guards! hang this villain on the battlements!

MES. Most gentle queen! my tale is not yet told.

JEZ. Then quick!—as long as thou hast breath to speak—
Ere that thy tale be strangled in thy throat!

AHAB (*aside*). Thy dauntless spirit should be lodged in me!
That which awakes the devil in her breast,
Has very nearly banished him from mine!
I breathe more freely that Elijah lives!

MES. This Gileadite is not a wight that can be caught.

JEZ. Ten thousand devils! Do you harp on that?

MES. Ah, how the tigress thirsts for human blood!—
Most gracious majesty, but hear me speak:
This Tishbite knave is one of the magicians—
A wizard, dealing with familiar spirits—
A sorcerer, a man of evil eye,
Who in an instant can transport himself
From Carmel unto Horeb, thence to Tyre.
Or Zidon, Egypt, or Jerusalem!
Of all the wandering Arabs I enquired,
And all were certain they had seen him late,—
Some here, some there, and all at once, as if
There were not one, but legions of Elijahs!

JEZ. Have I not said this Tishbite was a wizard—
A foul blasphemer, and a sorcerer?

AHAB. And, therefore, by our Law he ought to die!

JEZ. And so he shall—by Baal; so he shall!
Guards! seize this mole-eyed caitiff,—let him hang!

Our messengers must learn to use their wits,
Or be outwitted by a hempen cord!

        [*Exeunt* SOLDIERS *with prisoner.*

And now, my lord, break through this dismal gloom,
In which your clearer spirit is eclipsed.

AHAB. My life and joy! Whenever thou art near
A heavenly harmony steals o'er my soul,
Like that which lies concealed and unexpressed
In harp or lute, or sweetest dulcimer,
And only wakes when touched by cunning hands!

JEZ. Why then forego all customary use,—
Absent yourself from table,—steal away
From me and from our guests, as if you loathed
The sights and sounds you once delighted in?
Ah! you forget the past! you love me not!

AHAB. Forget the past!—forget my dearest life?
That were existence worse than death itself!
As well might I attempt to pluck the moon
From yonder sky, as thy fair image, Jezebel,
From the serene, unclouded firmament
Of past, imaginative life!—when love
Made thee my idol, and my joy for ever!

JEZ. Then hear me, if indeed I still remain
Your better genius and your faithful queen:
'Tis known that Naboth, spurning our decree,
Did shelter this Elijah when he fled;
Therefore the vineyard he denied for gold,
Is forfeit to the crown by legal right;
Nay, more—his life is forfeit to the law.

AHAB. Ha! but how? We have no witnesses?

JEZ. Art thou a King, and cry for witnesses!
All this I have forestalled—my way is clear:
I will proclaim a festival, at which
The elders and the nobles of Jezreel,
Our loyal lieges and most worthy friends,
Shall bear us witness Naboth had blasphemed

> God and the King;* and by our ancient law,
> The punishment of blasphemy is—*death!*

AHAB. Most true: I am remiss in zeal for God,
And in the cause of truth, since I forget
The laws and statutes of our ancestors.
This Naboth must be "stoned without the camp."

JEZ. So runs the statute law of blasphemy!

AHAB. Most excellent device! Ha, what? device!
Nay, nay! the law of God, the right of Kings,—
Both Heaven and Earth have championed my cause!
Amid the wild and strange antagonism
Of my conflicting thoughts, one rock remains
Steadfast, secure against all buffetings,
And flings the terror of the Prophet's† words
From me as if it were an idle dream,—
That rock on which my throne is firmly fixed,—
The statutes written in the Book of God!
How could I be so nice, so sensitive,
So tender and exceeding delicate,
As to forget the rights born with a King!
No more shall I with flesh and blood consult,
Or justify my actions to the world;
But with the voice that speaks from sceptred throne,
And by the argument of blood and iron!

JEZ. You speak right royally, and like a King,—
E'en with the spirit that befits a throne!
There is no virtue like a self-esteem.
'Tis only cowards that respect the world!
But come, I almost had forgot my charge:
Our friends are waiting in the festive hall,
And expectation stands on tiptoe for the King!
Remember it! my lord, remember it!—
That wine and woman's lips—runs it not so?—
Have lustier relish, tasted after—*blood!*
[*Exit.*

---

* EXODUS xxii, 28.

† Viz.: Elijah.

AHAB. Sweet is thy parting, Royal Jezebel,
    As the last smile of sunset o'er the sea!
    If all the stars should fight against me still,
    Let thou but shine on me with steady light,
    And I will follow thee, if thou should'st lead
    Into the very jaws of Erebus!
                        [*Exit* AHAB.

SCENE III.

AHAB's *Festive Hall.* *The King and Queen in State. Nobles, Priests of Astarte, Minstrels, &c.*

CHORUS (PRIESTS and MAIDENS.)

    Star of the Sea,*
      * Astarte.
    Lead me aright,
    Thou art to me
      Love and delight!
    Trusting in thee,
      Angel of light,
I fear not life's stormy ocean!
  Come in the twilight charm,
  When the heart is glowing warm,
Come when my spirit is wrapt in devotion!
  Heaven is around me then,
  When thy love thrills again,
Through the sweet pulses of life and of motion!
  Queen of the healing art,
  Come to my beating heart,—
Come like a summer calm over the ocean!

SONG (SOLO).

  Thou art sleeping, my Dearest,
    In beauty so bright,
  As the star now adorning
    The dark brow of night!

Not a thought but the purest
    Inhabits thy breast,
For the Angels who love thee
    Watch over thy rest!
Thou art lovely, my Dearest,
    As Dawn when she smiles
Through the sheen of her tresses
    On Emeral Isles!
There is not under heaven
    Of beauty so rare
As the brow of my Charmer
    In its dark flowing hair.
Sleep gently, my dearest,
    No whisper alarms,
Till Aurora's sweet blushes
    Shall blend with thy charms!
Ah! then we will wander
    Through woodland and grove,
And the warblers shall echo
    Our old song of love!

Chorus.

Hail, Ashtoreth! celestial queen of night!
  Dispense thy favours in thy mellowing beams;
Clothed in the purity of heavenly light
  Inspire in me the flame of love's ethereal dreams!
    Hail, goddess of the silver veil,
      Fair queen of love and harmony,
      And laughter-loving revelry,
    Before whose purer fire
      The hosts of heaven pale
  And disappear from the celestial choir!
For thee all hearts in concert beat,
    To thee our bosoms swell with pleasure,
When lip with lip in rapture meet
    And love without reserve or measure!

Song (Solo).

Then keep, O keep, the sacred vow
    Thy burning lips have sealed

With kisses passionate of love
    As made my soul to yield ;—
To yield in homage to thy charms,
    Rapt in the fires that play
In vestal brightness round those lips
    That mock the gates of day !

CHORUS.

Hail, pensive goddess, hornèd queen of Tyre,
    For thee the altar and the midnight flame
    Is lit by each Zidonian dame,
Whom thou hast ravished with thy vestal fire!
What time at pleasure's call their pulses beat,
And evening shades give birth to musings sweet ;
From thine eternal throne of rest
Thou hearest every sigh that heaves the breast.

SONG (SOLO).

Ah, wherefore dearest dost thou charm
    My soul with looks divine,—
And eyes in which the darts of love
    In cruel brightness shine !
If charms like thine are not for me,
    Spare me, ye shades of night!
Ah, still to dream that thou art near,
    In glancing beams of light!

CHORUS.

When summer clouds of saffron hue
    Curtain the chamber of the setting Sun,
And browsing cattle tread the falling dew,
    Or lie diffused upon the flowery plain,
And meditate their daily labour done,—
    I seek, O goddess, thy most sacred fane,
To offer thee my soul's desire,—
    The love which in my bosom yearns,
As warmly glowing as the vestal fire
    Which on thine altar burns !

Song (Solo).

Thy cheek is glowing in the tide
   Of passion's richest hue,
And love doth sparkle in thine eyes
   As light in morning dew !
The earth is fairer in thy smile,
   And birds more sweetly sing ;
And time itself in ecstasy
   Feels lighter on the wing !

Chorus.

When Phœbus sinks beneath the deep,
   And night sits on her ebon throne,
Decrepid age is gone to sleep,
   And youth and beauty wake alone
To watch the glimpses of the moon
   By crystal stream or magic grove,
And chide the hours that fly too soon,
   As they in loving converse rove !
The thrilling silence of each fairy scene,
   When Luna sits enthroned on high,
Unclouded and serene
   As Seraph's eye,
Is eloquent of feelings unexpressed,
   Of mute communion with the soul of things,
As when the pent-up raptures of the breast,—
   Fanning the bosom on ambrosial wings,—
   Find utterance in sweet imaginings !
And aye discourse their meaning in the face,
With more of eloquence and grace
Than speech can wed to harmony
In accents of divinest melody !
        [*Exeunt all, the* Chorus *singing.*

SCENE IV.

Horeb.—ELIJAH *sitting in a cave near the top of the mountain.*
Time—Midnight, same as last scene.

ELIJAH. Have mercy upon me, O Lord my God,
    For I am weak, and weary of this life!
    Have mercy on me, and forsake me not;
    Come to mine aid, or close mine eyes in peace!
    O, God! illume my soul, compel my thought,
    And save me from this hour!—So dark, dark, dark!
    O, Healer of all Sorrow! purge this ear
    So slow to catch a note of harmony
    Between my life and what it should have been,
    Between the concept, and the bringing forth!
    Full bitter were the pangs I did endure
    In giving scope to Heaven-aspiring thought;
    But now the sense of failure after toil
    Makes former agony a thrilling joy
    In the comparison!
    I have been zealous for Thee, Lord of Hosts,
    Yet may I not be, after all, a sound—
    A rustic piper, playing out of tune?
    Thou hast, O God, made all Thy creatures blest
    In the sweet intercourse of voice and song;
    The very birds that sing at heaven's gate
    Pour out their soul in artless song to Thee,
    And praise Thy Name; but man, alas, remains
    A note of discord in the general choir!
    And what am I? Alas! a wandering star,
    Blasting whatever comes within the sphere
    Of its dread orbit! Who can shew, O God,
    Ah, who can shew Thy people that they sin?
    Had not the Son of Beor light, yet stood
    On Pisgah's airy top to curse a race
    Ordained by Thee to be a people blessed?
    Had he not light who made the golden calf,
    And hailed it as the God of Israël?
    Had not the crownèd son of David light,
    And measured Wisdom by the Fear of God,

    Yet dallied with the goddess Ashtoreth?
    And who can shew that I, so full of zeal,
    May not relapse, by force of circumstance,
    Into the snare of Custom, and be found
    Among the rabble priests of Use and Wont,
    Who, in their ignorance, blaspheme Thy Name,
    Or wrest Thy Truth against the clearest light!
    Have I a clearer vision, stronger faith,
    Than other prophets had who toiled—and failed?
    Have I more light than they?

A Voice.   Not more!

Elijah.   Not more!
    Then who can teach Thy people righteousness?

Voice. What need has He of such a worm as thou?

Elijah. I have been jealous for the Lord of Hosts,
    Whose altars are thrown down, and prophets slain,
    By the blind worshippers of heathen gods!

Voice. Yet they who worship idols worship Him,
    And serve Him truly under many names!
    Thou hast mistook thy strength, and measured it
    With the Almighty Ruler of this world,
    Whose Government thou canst not understand
    Since thou art mortal, and canst only see
    A fragment of its infinite design!
    The evil thou pretendest to abhor
    Is but the necessary foil of good!
    Wouldst thou prefer an everlasting day
    To the harmonious interchange of light
    And shade? There is a unity which holds
    This universe of God in joint action!

Elijah. Then take away my life, or blot my name
    Out of thy book! for I have grieved for griefs
    Which are not mine, and thou hast heard me not!

Voice. Thou canst not change the fashion of the world;
    Then kneel before Despair and cease to be!
    Look back, and tell me what has been the prize
    Of those far greater men than thou, who fought

   Against the spirit of idolatry,—
   In common fashion or religious faith?
   Exile and bonds, imprisonment and death!
   And yet, blind fools!—they held that God is just;
   See how He deals with them that trust Him most!

ELIJAH. Better to be the outcast of the World
   Than be its slave! Whate'er THOU art, thy voice
   Comes not from Him, but from the pit of Hell!
   Approach, and show thy front!

    (TYPHON *now reveals himself*)

         If thou beest he
Who claimed the sovereignty of dire combustion
That night at Cherith when I vanquished thee,
Let all thine elements cry havoc now!
Set fire to Heaven and Earth—Scatter the hills,
Dash rocks to pieces, smite the mountains flat,—
Pluck up the world freighted with human woe,
And if thou canst, for thou art Sovereign Power,
Hurl it recking into its maker's face!
Art thou a Devil, and canst look amazed?
Thou cringing slave, thy sway is o'er the weak,
The melancholy, and the craven-hearted!
Yet canst not paralyse the feeblest knee
That bends in Secret prayer to the most High!
Where is thy thunder, Devil, and thy fire?
Let see which burns the hottest, thine or mine!
Thine has the greater torment; but in me
There burns a flame that would annihilate
The most rebellious spirit of the deep,
Yea, Hell itself, with all its mocking fiends!

TYPHON. Ha! ha! Thou hast blasphemed Him to His face,
   Who is thine enemy without a cause!
   But hearken—thou art just and innocent!
   Yet He laughs at the trials of the just!

ELIJAH. Vain tempter! thou wouldst have me in despair;
   Confound the words and works of God with thine!
   No doubt his Justice, Goodness, Holiness,

And truth. Avaunt!—thou hast no share in me,
Save in the smouldering dross of evil doubt
Innate through thine accursèd Victory
O'er the first Man, suspecting naught of guile!
And even that accursèd bond of sin,
Is severed in thy crushed defeat and fall!

TYPHON. Defeat and fall? I am His equal still,
Whereof my Victory is clearest proof!
Had not the Serpent taught thine ancestor,
His race would have remained as ignorant,
Unreasoning, servile, grovelling as the brutes;
But now they are, in thine own Master's words,
Become like gods, knowing both good and evil!
I have no share in thee? Ha! ha! What means
The bold ambition of thy restless mind,—
Thy scorn of vulgar ease and soft delights,
Thy proud defiance of His government,
Which works in contradiction to thy plan?
Dost thou not represent me in all this,
And justify the ground on which I stood,
When, challenging His arbitrary reign,
I erst rebelled against the Tyrant's creed,—
That disobedience is the cause of Sin;
And faith unreasoning, and servility,
The sole conditions of felicity?

ELIJAH. And to what height has thy ambition soared,
Or what has disobedience worked for thee?

TYPHON. To the inheritance of half His realms,
And the confusion of the other half!

ELIJAH. Alas! Too well I see the fruits of it;—
War, famine, plague, pestilence and death,
With thy most hellish brood of secret crime,—
Rape, incest, murder, theft, adultery,—
All rampant and luxuriant in the world,
Professed, abetted, and full oft confirmed,
By lawless Kings, and priests of such foul things
As Chemosh, Molech, Ashtoreth and Baal!
Behold this crop of thy dark work, and pray,—

For thou canst pray to thy confusion still,—
That God in mercy may annihilate
Thy being, or hide thee in the lowest deep!

TYPHON. Annihilate? No more than can Himself!
For I am portion of His very essence—
As real and as truly absolute
As th' emanation of His self-existence!
And as for darkness, what has that to do
With me? I in myself am light, and need
No sun, as mortals do, to shine for me!
What strange fatuity possesses man,
Who has become a god, forsooth! Ha! ha!
With all thy faith, self-sacrifice, and zeal,
Say, what hast thou effected in this world?
Another failure added to the list!
Then write it down where Moses wrote his law,
And die as he did of a broken heart!
Deserted and alone! unburied! lost!
Ah, fool! to throw away the nobleness,
The springtide and the blossom of thy life,
To make a bed of thorns for hoary age!
What cares the World for such a noisy trump
As thou art blowing in its stubborn ears?
Its pleasures are too sweet to be foregone
For visionary trifles of the brain,
More frequently the fumes of self-regard,
When Nature is surcharged with fortune's frown,
Than the inspirings of a healthy mind!
Return to Ahab; bend thy pride to him,
And from this lower round thou shalt ascend
To sit among the nobles of Jezreel!
It is thy nature to be great or nothing:
In this thou hast affinity with me!
'Tis only failure that makes life a sin—
Degree and honour are the seals of virtue!

ELIJAH. Degree and honour are but accidents,
Or baits to lure us from our better life;
And failure 'tis to worship them or thee!
The pleasures of the world are sweet, forsooth?

F

So was the apple! but the Serpent's sting
Soon made its virtues mortal. Ha! what next?

TYPHON. The pleasures of the flesh, I grant, are vulgar,
And have no charms for such a soul as thine;
But glory, fame, renown, are attributes
Of spirits tempered in celestial fire,
And fashioned in the likeness of the gods.
The noblest heroes of the Hebrew race
Were not content to hide their heads in caves,
Or waste their days in cursing gods and men;
They drew their swords to vindicate their faith,
And formed alliances with crownèd heads.

ELIJAH. O, doubly false is thy pernicious tongue,
Which ever tricks in specious eloquence
The deep damnation of thy fell intent!
It is thine art to be sophistical—
To trim a lie in fair seductive phrase,
And make confusion in the soul of man
By tempting him to sin in loving virtue!
If it may gratify thy hate to know,
Then hear the last that I shall answer thee:—
I am as great a sinner as thou art;
But I am saved, and thou for ever damned!

[TYPHON *fades away in the darkness, out of which a* VOICE *speaks.*

VOICE. To make thy desolation all complete,
Satan forsakes thee now as well as God!
But yet in parting He shall make thee feel
More terror than thy soul has ever known!

[*A flash of lightning and a terrible peal of thunder.*

The solid earth shall reel beneath thy feet!

[*The mountain shakes.*

The adamantine rocks, shattered and torn,
Shall fly before the tempest of my wrath,
And change to fearful meteors in the sky!

[*Meteors and fireballs fill the air.*

The rapid whirlwind, the devouring fire,

        The rending earthquake and the crashing thunder,
        Shall be my ministers to vent their ire
        On thy devoted head, and rend thy soul asunder!
                            [The storm rages.

ELIJAH. If the loud tempest dropping fire should rage,
        And with Destruction startle all the Orbs,
        I, unappalled, can bear the shock,
        And ride the blast triumphantly,
        On soaring pinions of my faith in God!
                            [Storm continues.

VOICE. The tempest breaks the rocks, the fragments fly
        Like shooting meteors through the mirky sky;
        As gusts of winds upon each other leap,
        And whirl the tossing foam from deep to deep!
        Thus when I breathe Destruction rules the World,
        And o'er the rack her banner is unfurled!

ELIJAH. How like the storm that gathers in my breast!—
        Loud,—terrible,—conflicting,—mutinous!
                            [Storm continues.

VOICE. The Earth shakes to and fro! and labouring still,
        The mountains roll like billows—hill on hill—
        Rising and falling with a horrid roar
        That rends the azure vault from shore to shore!
        The yawning chasms vomit fire and flame,
        And Nature trembles to her utmost frame!
        The fiery orbs start from their spheres on high,
        As if Destruction swept along the sky!
        The primal elements let loose again,
        Make chaos enter on a second reign!

ELIJAH. O Living Present! Thou that wilt endure,
        Unchangeable in Thy creative might,
        When like a dream the Nations of this Earth
        Yea, and the Earth itself, shall pass away,—
        Be near me in the terror of this hour,
        When Faith and Love are foundered in the dark,
        And shew me forth the virtues of mankind
        O'ertopping all the frailties I lament!

Reveal, O God, the purpose of my life,—
So seeming vain and frivolous to me,—
So barren of all fruit in Heaven's sight,
And O so weak and frail before Thy wrath
As frailest thing that shelters in the rocks,
And hides its head in covert from the Storm!

[*The storm dies away in the distance, and a soft
murmur falls on the Prophet's ear.*

Angelic Song.

Through the gleaming realms of azure
   Voices whisper, echoes fly;
And a murmur as of music,
   Falls in lulling melody!
Now the storm of passion over,
   With the mighty thunders roll,
Let the love of Heaven bless thee,
   And let peace possess thy soul!
See the rifted clouds are parting,
   And beyond are calmer skies,
Where the Angels now are tuning
   Harps responsive to thy sighs!
Bravely hast thou borne the conflict
   Few have felt and fewer stood;
When in darkness and forsaken,
   Hell went o'er thee like a flood!
Rise in triumph! faithful hearted!
   Thou hast conquered Death itself;
Thou hast saved a thousand others,
   Now thou hast redeemed thyself!

ELIJAH. An hour ago the ambient air was flame,
   Save when the Darkness swallowed it in Night;
   The Earth shook, trembling like a guilty thing;
   And 'twixt it and the clouds a horrid war
   Did threaten final Judgment! Now, methinks,
   An undertone of Love runs whispering by,
   And finds an echo in my heart! So let
   The jarring discord of rebellious thought
   Die like the far off thunder, and be lost

In the celestial strain of harmony!
I hear it still—and clearer than before,
As the soft lullaby of Nature's nurse,
To soothe the restless spirit of the Storm
And hush the tumult of my doubting heart!

> [ELIJAH, *wrapped in his mantle, stands at the entrance of the cave, and listens to the strains of* ANGELS *singing.*

ANGELIC SONG.

The voice of the tempest is o'er,
    And hushed is the storm, working fear;
The blast of the trumpet is blown,
    And the terrors of God disappear! *
When sorrow and mourning have ceased,
    Even they are with diadem crowned;
The darker the storms of the past,
    The brighter the glory they round!
The Angels of comfort return
    On glad and on passionate wing;
And on the mild Zephyrs of Dawn
    Ambrosial fragrance they fling!
With plumage unruffled by storms
    Around thee rejoicing they throng,
And on glances of tremulous light
    Make vocal the air with their song!

> [AZRIEL *descends in dazzling glory, and stands before* ELIJAH *still wrapped in his mantle.*

AZRIEL.† What doest thou here, Elijah? Speak!
    But look not on this blaze of Majesty;
    For Heaven's dazzling Light would blind and burn thee!

---

* EXODUS xix., 16, 19.

† I make Azriel here speak in the NAME of God, as I consider it the highest degree of presumption in any man to make the Almighty Himself one of the *Dramatis personæ*. Goethe makes himself painfully ridiculous in this respect; and even Milton sinks hopelessly beneath the weight of the task.

ELIJAH. I have been very jealous for the Lord
        Of Hosts; because the children of Israel
        Have forsaken Thy Covenant,
        Thrown down Thine Altars,
        And slain Thy prophets with the sword;
        And I, even I only, am left;
        And they seek my life to take it away!
        But what am I, Oh Lord,—a mortal man,—
        That I should hear Thy Voice, so terrible
        In Thy appearing!—

AZRIEL.   To those who fear Me not;
        But not to thee! Thou art mine own elect,
        And faithful still amongst a faithless race!
        I saw thee weep and watch the night, for sins
        Which were not thine; and thou hast thy reward!
        I saw thee drink the waters of affliction,
        Which into dews of peace are now distilled
        Upon the hearts of those whom thou hast taught,
        To soar above the shadows of this life,—
        Where Sin, Decay, and Death ride every blast,—
        Up to the Lovebeams of Beneficence,
        In which the Father's Face is radiant ever!
        'Tis not in scenes of triumph over crowds,
        Nor in the show of power miraculous,
        Such as made Ahab tremble on his throne,
        Thy life is seen by the Omniscient Eye
        Which tracks all time,—past, present, and to come;
        But in the hearts of those seven thousand men
        Still left in Israël, whom thou hast taught,
        In silent meekness, what is life indeed!
        Therefore the vanity and pomp of Kings,—
        Their temples, pyramids, and palaces,
        Shall fade away like visions of the night;
        But thou shalt live immortal as the Truth
        Thou hast revealed in discipline and love
        To all my Children, whilst the World remains!

ELIJAH. Thrice blessèd Comforter! Thy living words
        Are life indeed,—and rest unto my soul!—
        Now shall I die in peace, since Thou hast deigned,

O Lord, to glorify Thyself in me,
And sanctify my labour to Mankind!

AZRIEL. Thou art more highly favoured that the rest
Of all my servants here. Thou shalt not die,
But be received transfigured into Bliss,
When I have seen the mission of thy life
Fulfilled! Return into the Wilderness
Of old Damascus; and, when thou hast come,
Anoint Hazaël to be King of Syria;
And Jehu, son of Nimshi, King of Israël;
Elisha, him of Abel-Melholah,
Shalt thou anoint as prophet in thy stead.
Go! Meet the shock of things invisible;
And teach the future to unfold itself,
Until the nations of the World shall learn
That Sovereignty, in prophet or in King,
Consists in Consecration to MY WILL.

[AZRIEL *leaves* ELIJAH, *who has now learned the purpose of his life.*]

CHORUS OF ANGELS.

When the direful Archangel of Death,
    And his terrors swept over thy head,
Strong was thy faith in the Lord,
    Though lowly and rude was thy bed!
When the blast of his terrible wing
    Smote the Mountain of Horeb amain,
The death-dealing shaft of the foe
    Smote the heart of Elijah in vain!
The horror of darkness around,
    And the sound of the trumpet on high,
The rock-splitting tempest and flame,
    And the earthquake loud thundering bye,
Have left thee exalted in Faith,
    In the Name thou hast borne in the Strife—
Elijah!—El Yaveh!—the Strength
    Of Life!—from Eternity Life!
Alone thou hast battled with Sin,
    Alone thou hast ransomed the lost;

Alone thou hast witnessed to Truth,
  And alone thou hast suffered the cost!
One spirit like thine shall atone
  In the strength of its love for mankind,
When altars and victims shall fail
  To heal the deep wounds of the mind!
Thine be the peace and the joy,
  Unending, unsullied, and pure,
While angels attending thy steps
  Shall render thy future secure!
Until they shall greet thee on high,
  In the light of eternity blest,—
"Elijah, the Victor of Death!
  Now enter thy glorified Rest!"

FINIS.

PRINTED BY WALTER SMITH, 61 & 62, HIGH STREET, BLOOMSBURY, W.C.

www.ingramcontent.com/pod-product-compliance
Lightning Source LLC
Chambersburg PA
CBHW031608110426
42742CB00037B/1328